ISRAEL

Text by Carl Alpert

Crescent Books

Distributed by Crown Publishers, Inc.

View of Kiryat Shmona (in the distance, Mount Hermon).   Right, Jerusalem, a wall of the old Temple area.

Credits: Atlas: 83a - Braun-Clyne/Camera Press: 77 - 86b - Berne/Fotogram: 87a - Colomb/Atlas: 12a - Desgeorges/Atlas: 21a - 63b - 76 - 79b - Dulevant: 7a - 12b - 13 - 17a, b - 28b - 37 b - 41 - 57b - 62b - 66c - 67 - 84a - 91 - Dumas/Fotogram: 80a - Durand/Atlas: 21b - Fiore: 5 - 9b - 24 - 29a - 45 - 50a, b - 51 - 52 - 55 - 56 - 62a - 63a - 66b - 68 - 69b - 70 - 72a, b - 73 - 75b - 78 - 82b - 83b - 85 - 89a - Foucher-Creteau/Atlas: 58 - Len Sirman: 12c - 25c - 27b - 29b - 31b - 32 - 57a - 65a, b - 66a - 69a - 86c - 93b - Lenars/Atlas: 33 - Ministère du Tourisme-Jérusalem: 18b - 19b - 22b - 25a, d - 35b - 36 - 37a - 39 - 40 - 53 - 54b - 61 - 79a - 88 - 89b - Palphot: 2 - 9a - 10 - 11 - 18a - 19a - 20b - 22a - 28a - 42a, b - 48 - 49 - 74 - 75a - Petit/ Atlas: 7b - Picou/Fotogram: End-Papers: 6 - 26 - 46 - 47 - 54a - 59b - 60 - 82a - 93a - 94 - Pizzi/Gemini: 3 - 4 - 8 - 14 - 16b - 25b - 30 - 31a - 34 - 35a - 71 - 80b - 84b - 86a - 89c - 90 - 92 - 95 - 96 - Raspail/Atlas : 23 - Rechel/Camera Press: 81 - Sillner/Atlas: 84c - Tondeur/Atlas : 16a - 20a - 27a - 59a - 63c - 87b - Viollet: 1.

First English edition published by
Editions Minerva S.A., Genève
Library of Congress Catalog
Card Number: DS108.5.A69 956 79-9954
I.S.B.N. 0-517-28278-X
This edition is distributed by Crescent Books,
a division of Crown Publishers, Inc.

a b c d e f g h

1.

It is dangerous to dig anywhere in Israel. A farmer planning to put barren land into production may find that his plough has struck a tomb dating back to Bible times. In that case authorities at once prohibit all further work on the site until the archeological possibilities have been fully explored. It could take years.

A building contractor, plans in hand for a high rise office building, may find that his bulldozer has dug into a Roman mosaic floor. All work is frozen until the archeologists can determine if the location is to be declared a national monument.

Road builders, or engineers laying pipe lines, can all run into the same problem. As a result, exciting historic discoveries sometimes never get reported.

Even the casual visitor can play the game. During a stroll his foot may kick a Maccabean coin, a bit of Roman glass or a Crusader relic. Little wonder that some people keep their heads constantly bent earthward when walking on unpaved areas.

History began here about 8,000 years ago, and it has never stopped. This narrow strip of country, crossroads of the ancient world, is the bridge between Asia and Africa which every conqueror has had to cross. In recorded history it has prospered or suffered under the rule of the Amorites, Babylonians, Hyksos, Hittites, Philistines, Israelites, Assyrians, Greeks, Romans, Byzantines, Persians, Moslems, Crusaders, Mamelukes, Turks and British. The latest stage began with the establishment of the State of Israel in 1948.

It has been a land of sharp contradictions ever since Joshua sent the Biblical spies as members of the country's first Investigation Commission. One report: "A land flowing with milk and honey". And: "A land that devours its inhabitants.

Those who retain their Sunday School image of the Holy Land will look for the camels, the stately cypress trees, the Bedouin tents. They will find all these, but sometimes in startling proximity to twentieth century industry in the form of aircraft manufacturing plants, nuclear reactors, or sophisticated textile factories. They will inhale the sweet odors of orange groves in blossom, seen faintly through the haze created by the smoke from the cement factory.

There are mountains and valleys, tropical plantations and deserts. And there are rocks. Why is the Holy Land so rocky? There is an old Jewish story to the effect that every Jewish pilgrim who had come to the land through the centuries had by such visit lightened his historic burden — figuratively, dropped a stone from his heart. It is the accumulation of these stones that give large parts of the country, in the north and the Judean hills, their characteristic appearance. But scientists at the Technion are working on a system to bring benefit to mankind by reaching the oil in the shale rock and thus providing the energy that civilization requires. Moses struck the rock with his staff and produced water. Modern science uses the laser beam.

It is said that in this land one who does not believe in miracles is not a realist. In ancient times the miracles were unexplained phenomena. Today they are man-made. The pace is frenetic. Even siestas, it appears, are taken energetically. Israelis characterize the pace themselves: That which is extremely difficult, they say, can be done quickly. The impossible may take a little longer.

2.

If first impressions are important there is no better introduction to Israel than Haifa. In quick comparison it has been likened to Rio de Janeiro, Naples, Cape Town, San Francisco. But it is like these only in its topographical siting as a city built on the side of a hill sloping down to the sea. Haifa has a character of its own.

Like ancient Gaul it is divided into three parts. First is the lower town, centred around the port, a busy, bustling, hustling commercial area. Businessmen and shipping agents rub shoulders with sailors and street peddlers who display their imported sundries along the sidewalks of what used to be known in the days of the British Mandate as Kingsway, but now bears the proud name of Derech Ha-Atzmaout — Independence Road. One inconspicuous alley leads to a colorful, crowd-

Above, general view of Haifa looking inland. Facing, the Bahai Shrine. Right , a station in the Carmelit, Haifa's underground cable-car.

ed fruit and vegetable market, typical of those found in most Israel towns. The broad road bears heavy truck traffic, and few visitors are aware that forty years ago this entire area lay under water. The land was reclaimed by the British as part of the port development program. Today Israeli engineers are busily at work reclaiming even more land from the bay. Sand dredged up from the deep ship channels is pumped on the coast outside the port, and the land area of Israel grows from month to month. Numerous luxury liners make Haifa a regular port of call on Mediterranean cruises. In season there are scores of freighters at any one time loading the citrus crop for European and more distant markets.

That functional commercial buildings need not necessarily be eyesores is demonstrated by the graceful lines of the Dagon grain elevators, con-

spicuously located at the waterfront. Near the eastern exit from the city is a strange-looking monument, a single marble pillar, which appears to have been abruptly snapped off in the middle. It was set up in this way by the Arabs in 1935 in memory of Feisal, former King of Syria and Iraq, who had been deposed by the French. It symbolizes his broken glory. The Arabic inscription on the base reads: "Independence is not given; it must be seized. A nation's freedom is in its own hands."

Haifa's second section is half way up the mountain and is known as Hadar Hacarmel (Glory of the Carmel). It contains the main retail shopping streets, lower middle class residential areas, public institutions, and off to one side the beautiful gardens and buildings of the Bahai faith. Haifa is the world headquarters of the Bahai, for it

6

was here, more than a hundred years ago, that Baha'u'llah, leader of the faith, finally found haven after exile from his native Persia. The beautiful gold dome, one of the outstanding landmarks on Haifa's hillside, surmounts the old stone building in which are interred the remains of the Bab, the forerunner of the faith. The shrine is thus a mausoleum, and not a Temple as it is often erroneously called.

Haifa's third section is on the upper slopes and on the long strip of plateau which extends along the crest of Mount Carmel. From Yefe Nof (Panorama) Road the visitor not only looks down upon the city immediately below, but also has a splendid and exciting vista. The eye follows the blue curve of Haifa Bay around to the ancient city of Acre, then up the coast to the white cliffs of Rosh Hanikra, marking the border with Lebanon. The hills of Galilee provide the backdrop. The graceful symmetrical twin concrete cooling towers of the oil refinery constitute a dominating landmark. The less romantic observer may be more conscious of the smoke belching from the stacks of the various industrial enterprises which have multiplied in the flatlands around the Bay. At night the twinkling lamps of the city and the clusters of lights from villages up in the mountains — patches which seem to hang in mid-air — make the scene an unreal fairyland. On Saturdays the Bay is dotted with several score sailboats.

It was here, on Panorama Road, that Kaiser Wilhelm II stood in 1898, looked down upon the red-tiled roofs of the colony of German Templars who had settled in Haifa, and perhaps dreamed his dreams of a Berlin to Bagdad railway, and the *Drang nach Osten.* An obelisk commemorating the visit was erected by the Templars. When General Allenby's soldiers occupied the city in

1918 they effaced the German inscription, and the monument stands today, a forlornly unidentified and almost forgotten relic of a bygone day.

The upper Carmel is the site of lovely homes, high rise hotels, gemütlich cafes and pensions, parks and the impressive campuses of the Technion, Israel Institute of Technology, and Haifa University. At any level, a visitor may enter the Carmelit, proudly identified as the only Subway in the Middle East. It is an underground cable car which runs from the top of the mountain down to Paris Square, at the port level, making in some eight minutes a run which buses, travelling the zig-zag roads, require almost half an hour to traverse. But of course one can not see the city from underground. The roads snake back and forth up the face of the hill, giving the car rider his beautiful view, now from the left and then, after a turn, again from the right.

The Carmel slopes are broken by a series of ravines, or wadis, and numerous independent ridges jut out from the mountain line. The result is a challenge to Israel's architects. They have solved the problem by building apartment houses, almost all condominiums, staggered like steps up and down the hill, the roof of one flat serving as the extended terrace of the apartment above. There can be as many as eight of these steps.

Haifa has its own theater, its own symphony orchestra and other cultural attractions, chief among them a network of museums dealing with archeology, modern art, music, ethnological groups, Japanese art, maritime and nautical interests, and even a museum devoted to the illegal immigration when Jewish refugees from Europe's Displaced Persons camps sought to avoid the British blockade. This museum is housed in a beached ship which actually made the run.

But Haifa has been termed by its devotees and critics alike a sleeping beauty. There are no night clubs of distinction, few bars and restaurants of the type that cater to tourists, indeed, little to do at night except rest up for the exciting day to follow.

When the United Nations provided for establishment of a Jewish State in 1947 the surrounding Arab lands refused to recognize the decision and declared war on the infant democracy. In Haifa, Jews and Arabs had long lived together in peaceful harmony. Uncertain of the future, many Arabs began to leave. Their Jewish neighbors urged them to remain, assuring them all would be well. Unfriendly agitation stirred up the fears, and the Arab departure became a mass flight. By the time the British formally withdrew from Palestine, Haifa came under Israel rule. There was very little fighting in the city, and the Arabs who remained have had no cause to regret their decision. They may live anywhere in Haifa, though many are concentrated in the lower city and in the Wadi Nisnas area. The visitor will see first in Haifa a phenomenon common to all of Israel's cities: the street signs are in three languages, Hebrew, Arabic, English.

Within the city limits is the Arab village of Kababir which maintains its separate identity as a social enclave though modern, Jewish Haifa has crept right up to its borders. Diligently the villagers, who are for the most part employed in constructing some of the city's fine homes, are gradually rebuilding their own village. Lovely villas are beginning to emerge from the old stone shacks.

As a glance at a map will show, Haifa is a peninsula jutting out to sea. From many places at the top of the mountain one has a view of water on

Left, administration building of the Technion, Institute of Technology. The boat shown opposite houses the Illegal Immigration Museum. Below, Mount Carmel as seen from the Bahai Gardens.

both sides. At the furthest northwest extremity of the promontory the foot of the mountain is literally washed by the waves of the sea, with just about enough room left for a road and the railroad line. Atop the hill is the monastery of the Carmelites, an Order said to have been founded by the Prophet Elijah, but more formally established in the year 1156. The present building is one in a succession of structures on this site. Beneath the altar is a cave which is associated with the Carmelites' patron, Elijah. Some six hundred feet down at the foot of the mountain is another cave, this one identified by the Jews with the prophet. He could well have had two or more homes.

Outside the monastery is a pyramidal monument and an iron cross serving as a memorial to Napoleon's soldiers who were killed during the ill-fated siege of Acre. One of the minor incidents here during the early years of the First World War was when the monument was violated, allegedly at the instigation of local Germans. In retaliation, a French warship steamed into the harbor and shelled the home of the German Consul. The memorial was quickly restored.

Undoubtedly the oldest street in Haifa is Stella Maris Road, built by the first Carmelites to enable donkeys and pilgrims to climb the side of the hill from sea level up to the Monastery. Today it is widened and paved, and carries more rapid traffic.

Further inland, on the highest parts of the Carmel, are the Druze villages of Isfiyah and Dalia el'Carmel. There are about 40,000 Druzes in Israel and about 300,000 in Syria and Lebanon. The Druzes follow a monotheistic religion, an offshoot of Islam, theological details of which are kept secret and are known only to the leaders of the community. Their chief prophet is Jethro, Biblical father-in-law of Moses. Their language is

9

Arabic, but they are not Moslems and through the centuries have had to struggle to maintain their separate identity. Their farmlands dot the stony sides of Carmel ridges, but the green-thumbed Druzes today find it more profitable to serve as gardeners for the proliferating Jewish homes on the mountain. Nearby is Mukhreka, legendary site of the duel fought by Elijah with the false prophets of Baal, as described in the First Book of Kings. A Carmelite monastery today marks the spot, alongside an imposing statue of the Prophet.

Mount Carmel is not a peak, but a range approximately twenty miles long, stretching east and south of Haifa. A few miles south of the city, nestling in a curve of the hill, is the village of Ein Hod, a bohemian and creative home for distinguished Israeli artists as well as for promising new young talents. The old hills contain numerous caves, some of which show unmistakable evidence of occupancy by Stone Age man. The contemporary tourist may wander into the caves where bones and artifacts of Paleolithic man have been found. Further south, still on the Carmel, is the quiet town of Zichron Yaakov, founded in 1882. The famous wine cellars are open to visitors, and the hosts are generous in offering tastes of their vintage.

At the very southern tip of the Carmel, as it descends to sea level flatland, are the remains of the old Roman aqueduct which carried water from the Carmel springs, by gravity flow, to the metropolis of Caesarea. Excavations have revealed only a small part of the city which, during Roman times, eclipsed Jerusalem as the political and commercial center of the land. The old Roman theater, fully uncovered and retouched, is today a popular and exotic site for concerts and dramatic performances, with the Mediterranean serving as a backdrop. The ancient elliptical hippodrome is obvious, but still awaits full excavation. For miles around broken marble pillars poke up out of the sand. Farmers' ploughs time and again bite into mosaic floors or other remnants of the far-flung Roman capital.

At the sea, alongside the ruins of the port built by Herod, are remains of the fortifications put up by the Crusaders when they held sway over the area. The visitor can clamber back through time, from Crusader to Roman to the even older Phoenician remnants on the site. In this vicinity the Israelis have built a luxury hotel, a golf course and a suburb of exclusive, attractive villas.

The sands from the waterfront, or elsewhere from the desert, reach inland and are fought by the farmers. The desert can be reclaimed, but where there is neglect the sands creep in again, like a moving crystalline glacier. And there are trees. The sanctity of the holy places associated with the various religions is matched only by the sanctity attached to trees in Israel. In ancient times large sections of the country were heavily forested. Depredations of the grazing goats, careless use of timber to fire the Turkish trains, and general indifference gradually resulted in denuding vast areas. Restoration of the woods has become a secular religion. Children in the schools are taught to revere trees. A special holiday marks tree-planting time. There are sites where tourists can plant trees with their own hands, and get a certificate attesting to their horticultural skill. Municipal ordinances forbid the chopping down of trees except by special permit. Bit by bit sections of Israel are again being carpeted with green woods. The extensive Carmel forests are typical of what will be found elsewhere in Israel. The extremes of altitude and temperature

Left, "Elijah's Cave" under the altar of the Carmelite Monastery. Below, Mount Carmel pock-marked by caves of primitive man.

dictate the genus, but the variety includes pine, oak, carob, palm, cypress, terebinth, acacia and groves of citrus, apples, pears, peaches, dates and olives. The Australian eucalyptus, introduced to help drain the swamps, has acclimated itself and grows rapidly. The National Park Authority and the Jewish National Fund have set up wooded picnic areas, or general reserves where nature is encouraged, with a little help, to take over once again.

Above, ruins on the site of Caesarea. Below, Roman aqueduct at Caesarea. Right, ancient olive tree on the road to Haifa. Right, remains of Roman art in Caesarea.

3.

The road north from Haifa leads around the bend of the Bay, through an area which within the memory of living man was a malarial swamp. Today neat workmen's homes and modern industrial plants fill the suburbs. Occasionally a dense lowland fog covers the plain, reminding us that nature had other plans for the place. The swamps have been drained and the water flows quietly and innocently through two creeks which come down from the mountains and empty into the sea.

The first is the historic Kishon, famed in Bible story, which ran red with the blood of Israel's enemies in the time of Deborah the Prophetess and again in the days of Elijah the Prophet. Today the leisurely Kishon fights pollution from another source, for chemical plants line its shores. The mouth of the Kishon has been widened and deepened so that it serves as an auxiliary to the Port of Haifa. Here is a fisherman's cove, the yachting basin for Haifa's sailboat enthusiasts, and a very respectable shipyard. One report has it that the original enlargement of the Kishon Port in the early 1950's was to create a free port area for use of the Jordan Government, when peace came about with that country. Lacking any outlet to the Mediterranean, Jordan was expected to be receptive to the offer, and Israel prepared accordingly.

The second creek is even more modest, and in the dry season does not always have water. The Naaman/Belus "river" outlet is, according to tradition, the site of the accidental discovery of glass. A ship carrying a cargo of rock rich in

Section of the seawall at Acre.

sodium was wrecked on this Phoenician shore. The sailors huddled around a makeshift fireplace on the sands, made with stones from their cargo. In the flames the sodium combined with the silicate on the beach and in the morning the sailors discovered globs of glass in the ashes. It is a fact that hardly a year goes by without a ship's running ashore here, victim of the winds and currents in the bay.

At the further end of the bay is Acre, known in ancient times as Ptolemais. When there was nothing at Haifa but a tiny fishing village, this was the main port and capital of the province. It was perhaps the major center during the period of Crusader influence in the country. St. Francis of Assisi landed here and introduced the Franciscan Order.

There are many remnants of the Crusader occupancy, including the old City Wall on the sea side, and a huge underground chamber first erroneously identified as the Crypt of St. John, but later recognized as the knights' refectory. It possesses excellent acoustical properties and is frequently used for chamber music concerts. Much of old Acre can be seen underground, connected by tunnels and passages which have been excavated and cleaned up. Acre's last major claim to fame was in 1799 when Napoleon's thrust to the East reached here. In that year Bonaparte's invading army came up from Egypt, conquered Gaza, Ramla, Jaffa and Haifa, only to be stopped at Acre. He had issued a proclamation promising the Jewish people living in 2,000 years of exile that he would restore them to the land of their forefathers, but he was never in a position to keep that promise. For 61 days his troops laid siege to Acre, but the Turks held out and he was forced to withdraw. The heights nearby, where he mount-

ed his inadequate artillery, are to this day known as Napoleon's Hill. Another Napoleon's Hill is outside Jaffa.

The Arabs who built here in the Middle Ages found a ready source of building materials at the ruins of Caesarea, down the coast, and much of the marble embedded in Acre's old structures was once floated to the city on rafts from the former Roman capital. The major Arab monument is Jazzar's Mosque. During the days of the Mandate over Palestine the British maintained a security prison in Acre and many of Israel's national heroes once served time within those walls. A major prison break was engineered from the outside by the Jewish underground in 1947. Today occasional art bazaars and exhibitions are held in what used to be the Turkish khan. Arab fishermen sit in the sun and mend their nets. At night the lighthouse blinks its warning to craft at sea. Acre is quaint and colorful, but a city of the past. Modern housing has now extended the city limits far beyond the old walls.

The road continues north up the coast, punctuated by small colonies and settlements. One of the unique villages is Nes Ammim, founded largely by Dutch Christians, and dedicated to a renewal of Jewish-Christian cooperation on a wholesome, non-missionary basis. A number of other English-speaking settlers have joined them. The little Christian children here speak Hebrew, and in the local schools observe the Jewish holidays.

Above: the ramparts of St John of Acre, by the sea, and the El Jazzar Mosque. Facing and right, a caravan hosterly and fisherman's cove.

16

*The beach at Nahariyah.
Bottom, sea and cliffs at Rosh Hanikra.*

Nahariya was founded in 1934 largely by Jewish refugees from Germany. They gave the town such an unmistakably German stamp that when an early U.N. investigating commission proposed partitioning Palestine into a Jewish State and an Arab State, with Nahariya to be included in the latter, people were advised not to worry. No matter where it is located, they said, *Nahariya bleibt immer Deutsch.*

The border with Lebanon is reached at Rosh Hanikra (Ras Al Naqura) whose chalky limestone cliffs can on clear days be seen from Mount Carmel. There is much traffic through the international gate: U.N. vehicles, diplomatic personnel and clergy. The border point and observation posts are high up on the promontory, but a short cable car ride takes the visitor down to the grottoes where the blue-green waters of the Mediterranean beat and splash into the caves, and the light dances on the ripples and is reflected back onto the worn stone walls. The rusted and abandoned old railroad tracks which once ran from Haifa through these grottoes to Beirut serve as reminders of recent history.

The Galilee hills stretch to the east. In this area, as well as in other parts of Israel, will be found that unique form of social organization known as the kibbutz (plural, kibbutzim). It has long been the object of curious attention and sociological research. The first kibbutz was established at Degania, on the lower tip of the Sea of Galilee, in 1909 when a group of Jewish *halutzim* (pioneers) felt that by pooling their talents, efforts and means in a voluntary collective they would have a better chance of conquering the soil and making their settlement succeed. The kibbutz was to be a model of social equality. For many it was a way to realize the Zionist revolution in Jewish life

18

which sought not merely to set up a Jewish state, but also to change the social and vocational stratification of the Jewish community. Labor Zionism preached that there was dignity in manual labor and in agriculture. If the Jews were to be a normal people like all other nations, they must have their own farmers and proletarians. A basic principle of the kibbutz was self-labor. The very idea of hiring assistance smacked of exploitation.

Today there are some 230 kibbutzim located in all parts of the country. Some of the newer ones are still in the semi-primitive state of the first experimenters. Many of the older colonies have become settled, prosperous, and while they are still collective in principle, have assumed somewhat bourgeois characteristics. More than half the income of the kibbutzim now comes from industrial operations. The first plants were based on processing and preserving of the agricultural products, but now one finds heavy metal product plants, electronics and science-based factories, building materials, machinery, indeed, almost every field of technological production. Economic realities have made it necessary to bend the original ideals, and in some kibbutzim hiring of outside labor has reluctantly been put into effect. Though they account for little more than 2% of the population of the country, the kibbutzim have produced many of the country's political and military leaders. Their influence on Israel has been far greater than their numerical proportion.

It is not as easy to visit a kibbutz as it used to be. Overwhelmed by growing numbers of curiosity seekers, many of the settlements have capitalized on this interest and have set up guest houses, clean, comfortable, with good food and modest prices. Thus a new industry has come to the farm. Among the many kibbutz guest houses in the

19

northern part of the country three may be singled out for special mention. One is Gesher Haziv, just south of Rosh Hanikra; Kfar Blum (named for France's Leon Blum) up in the northeast corner, alongside the Jordan River; and Ayelet Hashachar (Morning Star), some miles to the south.

Not all of Israel's agriculturists live in kibbutzim. There are many private farmers. The moshav, a cooperative village, is also a popular form of organization. It retains much of the cooperative aspects of the kibbutz in field work, joint purchasing and marketing, but each family lives its own private life and manages its own finances. Moshe Dayan was for some years a farmer in one such Moshav, Nahalal. Arab farms produce most of Israel's tobacco, barley, melons and sesame seed, but contribute also to the supply of vegetables and fruit. Many Arab farms are highly mechanized and use sophisticated irrigation methods, but it is not unusual to see old fashioned, animal-drawn ploughs and antiquated methods of separation of grain from the chaff. The Galilee hills are to a large extent very rocky, and one must admire the farmers, Arab or Jewish, who have learned to apply modern science to their agriculture and to scratch more than a bare living from the forbidding looking wastes.

There are surprises at every turn. At one point it might be an expanse of gnarled and ancient olive trees, nurtured by successive generations of Arabs. At the next turn are the impressive remnants of the 2nd-3rd century synagogue at Bar'am. Later one finds the modern city of Kiryat Shmona set up close to the border with Lebanon. Nearby is the rugged stone statue of the Lion of Judah, commemorating the pioneers led by Joseph Trumpeldor who were killed at Tel Hai in 1920 in defense of their homes. In the muddled period following the

collapse of the Ottoman Empire it was not clear whether this neighborhood belonged in the French sphere of influence with Lebanon, or in the British area, with Palestine. The heroic stand by Trumpeldor and his colleagues established the projecting thumb of land as part of Palestine. The hills climb higher, up the slopes of snow-covered Mount Hermon, where the Israelis have built a ski-lift, and on to the great fertile plateau of the Golan Heights, occupied by Israel since 1967. Modern Jewish settlements have proliferated and remains of ancient Jewish settlements have been uncovered everywhere.

Not far away—everything in little Israel is close

Above, view of Mount Hermon. Below and right, contrasting views of Lake Tiberias.

—lies the picturesque city of Safed. Its history is reflected in a queer mixture of Roman fortifications, 16th century synagogues where the *Kabbala,* Jewish mysticism, reached its apex, a crazy-quilt pattern of tilting ruins which are the remnants of the heavy earthquake of 1837, and a contemporary colony where some scores of modern artists have set up studios and galleries. The combination of gorgeous mountain vistas and the almost perceptible feeling of the history with which the whole place is saturated, provides artistic stimulation. Still another unique place is the little hamlet of Amirim, said to be the only successful all-vegetarian village in the world. The healthy farmers take in boarders, too.

In this area is the highest mountain in Israel (1208 meters) the Jermak, also known as Mount Meron. Here was the centre of a flourishing Jewish religious and cultural life in the second and third centuries; holy tombs abound. On the spring festival of Lag B'Omer thousands of religious Jews stream to the tomb of Rabbi Shimon Bar Yochai and spend the night in an ecstasy of worship through song and dance. Nearby is a stone doorpost with a cracked lintel, said to be the remnant of a 1700-year-old synagogue. There is an oft-repeated legend that when the lintel falls, the Messiah will come. The Government, in its desire to preserve the old relic, has bolstered and strengthened the broken stone. In this way, the cynics say, the secularists assure that the Messiah's coming will be delayed.

At turns in the road one gets first glimpses of the shimmering waters of the Sea of Galilee (also known as Lake Tiberias) lying far below, some 600 feet (200 meters) below sea level. Israelis call it in Hebrew *Kinneret,* from the Hebrew word for harp, whose shape the lake is said to resemble.

The ribbon of road winds its way down almost precipitously and ends up in the lakeside city of Tiberias, which still bears the name of the emperor who ruled in Rome when it was first built. The entire surrounding area is drenched in Biblical history, especially of the New Testament. This is where Jesus walked the waves in the wind. The modern visitor may indeed see a sudden and violent wind storm break out on the placid waters of the Lake. This is where the Fisherman cast his nets, and the tasty catch served in restaurants on both sides of the Kinneret are to this day called St. Peter's fish. On these shores are the carefully preserved ruins of the old synagogue at Capernaum (Kfar Nahum) where Jesus is said to have worshipped. Tradition has it that the hill close by is the Mount of the Beatitudes where Jesus gave utterance to the memorable teachings: "Blessed are the poor in spirit; for theirs is the kingdom of Heaven. Blessed are the meek; for they shall inherit the earth..."

Left, the town of Tiberias, the lake and, in the background, the Golan Heights. Above, two faces of the seaside resort established at Tiberias. Below and right, remains of Capernaum, where Christ preached.

Left, the Mount of Beatitudes (or of the Sermon on the Mount), in Galilee. Above, a section of the Jordan River. Below, one of the headwaters of the Jordan.

Tiberias is earthquake prone, as is the whole rift running from the north of the country down the Jordan Valley to the Dead Sea. The black, basalt rock, from which many structures are built, including the ruins of the Crusader fort jutting out into the waters of the Sea, give evidence of the once active volcanoes here. Further evidence is to be found in the hot mineral springs which still emerge undiminished from the hillsides and provide the foundation for a thriving industry of health spas.

The lake may be circumnavigated by car on good roads, or crossed by boat. On the eastern shore is Ein Gev, a kibbutz founded in 1937, and known today for such mixed attractions as its fish dinners, its tropical fruits and its annual music festival. The puny stream of the Jordan empties into the Sea of Galilee in the north, and emerges at the southern end with some reinforcement. Despite the fame which it has achieved in history and in spiritual songs, the Jordan is not the mighty torrent which some might expect. It is at best a lazy creek, in places with rocky rapids, a rivulet, and at some times easily fordable.

27

A road winds up the hill near the center of the Lake, heading toward what looks like a mountainous saddle. These are the twin peaks of the Horns of Hittin. On this plain, in the year 1187, Saladin at the head of his Moslem forces inflicted on the Crusaders the massive defeat which brought about the end of the Christian kingdom in the Holy Land. The fields are peacefully tilled by the farmers of the religious kibbutz, Lavi, which also operates a Guest House.

Almost everywhere in Israel the military events and the wars of the past have their parallel in the military presence of today. Israel's soldiers frequently take their guns home with them on leave. Men in uniform are to be found hitch-hiking all over the country, and most motorists will stop to give soldiers a lift. Hitch-hiking is not forbidden; to the contrary, official "tremping" stations have been set up at major intersections to facilitate the rides. In Israel the military is a citizens' army. Everyone is subject to conscription at the age of 18, and men serve for three full years, girls somewhat less. After completion of the required period of service, every soldier is in the reserves and is called up annually. Officers in the armed forces are usually retired before the age of 50, thus making a pool of managerial talent available to industry, but also keeping the army young and on its toes.

Arab villages predominate in the lower Galilee, among them Kafr Kana, where Jesus performed his first miracle, turning water into wine. A few miles away is Nazareth, where Jesus spent thirty years, unknown and then misunderstood and rejected. The new Church of the Annunciation, many years in the building, is faithful to the spirit and architecture of its predecessors on the same site. There are churches of all denominations, and

28

Left, the Jordan. In Nazareth: facing, detail of the church of the Annunciation. Below, general view of the city and, bottom left, a market in one of its streets.

Mount Tabor.

a Mosque of Peace. A new development on the neighboring hill, Nazareth Ilit, is almost exclusively a Jewish suburb.

Once again the visitor descends from the mountain, this time to the broad Valley of Jezreel, known today in Hebrew simply as the Emek, the Valley. The great highways of history, over which travelled the merchant caravans or the invading armies, north and south, traversed this plain. This is the site of the traditional Armageddon, but today it is peaceful and pastoral. Jewish settlers began to reclaim the Emek from its desolation fifty years ago. They drained its swamps and transformed it into the granary of Israel. The neatly cultivated fields, whether of grain, cotton, or fodder, sometimes stretch almost to the horizon. Cotton did we say? A quarter century ago the crop was tried here for the first time. It failed, and the experts gave up. A successful plantation owner from southern California, Sam Hamburger, insisted on trying again, with his seeds and his methods. In a short period of time it has become a miracle crop, producing long staple cotton in almost every part of the country. Today Israel grows all the cotton it needs for local use, and has enough left over for export. The success story has given renewed hope.

One broad stretch of the Emek can be crossed from west to east on a long road which extends as straight as a ruler. And so it is known as the *sargayl*, the ruler. The Emek is bounded by historic highlands. Here is Mount Tabor, scene of the Transfiguration. Perched high atop the perfectly dome-shaped peak is a Franciscan monastery.

The narrow road twists its way up the mountain side in a succession of almost terrifying hairpin turns. The veteran driver-guides usually seek to reassure their passengers as the cars maneuver the narrow curves by telling them: "Keep calm. Just do as I do, close your eyes!"

On the other side of the Emek are the slopes of Mount Gilboa, where King Saul fell tragically in battle. Further along are the fortifications at Megiddo, which commanded the strategic passes entering the Valley. Here successive powers built their cities which were conquered and razed and rebuilt by new invaders. A huge cross section cut into the *tel*, the accumulated mound of the centuries, revealed no less than twenty layers of civilization beginning with the Bronze Age, through ancient Egyptian dynasties, Biblical kings including David and Solomon, the Assyrians, the Persians, right down to our own times. General Allenby came through the Megiddo pass in 1918 and defeated the Turks, whereupon the Ottoman control of the country crumbled.

At its western extremity the Emek rises again into the back of the Carmel range. In the 1930's archeologists found at Beth Shearim not only the remains of a once flourishing Jewish town from the Second and Third Centuries, but a breathtaking necropolis, a huge complex of catacombs which are dug into the soft limestone hills and create the feeling of a vast underground city of the dead. The sarcophagi, epitaphs and coins found here cast considerable light on the life of the Jews during the centuries following the Roman destruction of their holy Temple in the year 70 A.D.

The entrance to the catacombs at Beth Shearim and, below, the Roman theatre at Beth Shean.

4.

The road system is generally good, and there are major highways linking the main cities. Private cars have multiplied in recent years but mass transportation is by bus, which provides cheap, efficient and frequent service to every corner and every outpost of the land. For passenger traffic the railroad has not been able to compete with the buses, but on the rail trip between Tel Aviv and Jerusalem there are numerous unforgettable views in the mountains.

What is today the heart and center of Israel's population was once the town of Jaffa, one of the oldest cities in the world. The rocks just off shore are where Andromeda was chained, according to Greek legend, and from which she was rescued by Perseus. It was from Jaffa that Jonah set sail on his ill-fated voyage that ended up inside a whale. The city was also the home of such varied historical personalities as St. Peter, Simon the Tanner and Godfrey of Bouillon. Archeologists have only begun to scratch the surface of the rich historical potential. For centuries Jaffa served as the main port of the country. In 1909 some of the Jewish inhabitants bought the sand dunes stretching along the beach north of the city, built a residential suburb, and named it Spring Hill—

Left, general view of Tel Aviv. Below, the city center, at down, around Rothschild Boulevard.

Facing, another view of Tel Aviv, the name of which means Spring Hill.

Tel Aviv. The city grew, at first with little planning, and the result was an urban jungle. According to one account the first "master plan" called for streets laid out in the shape of the traditional menorah, the seven-branched candelabrum. This led to traffic chaos. Eventually scientific town planning sought to regulate the municipal growth. Today the Tel Aviv sprawl includes old Jaffa within its municipal limits and encompasses, at least geographically, half a dozen other cities and towns which are contiguous with it. Almost a third of the country's population is concentrated in this megalopolis.

Like any large, modern city, Tel Aviv is many-faceted. Visitors who spend a day exploring it may compare notes in the evening and find that their impressions are as different as those of the blind men feeling the elephant. Many see in Tel Aviv, with some justice, the cultural center of Israel. In 1936 a refugee conductor, Bronislaw Huberman, gathered a group of musicians, many of them also refugees from Europe, and formed what became the Israel Philharmonic Orchestra. Subscription tickets to its concerts are constantly at a premium, and world famous conductors frequently appear on its podium. Its "at home" concerts are given in the Mann Auditorium, but it also travels throughout Israel, and makes frequent trips abroad. There are several theatrical companies, best known of which is Habimah. The highest attendance rate per capita in the world for theatrical performances and music concerts is registered in Israel.

Museums present exhibitions of modern art, Mediterranean culture, glass art and many other subjects. The love of beautiful things has also influenced the production of Israel's postage stamps, many of which are regarded as works of

*Tel-Aviv: the City Hall,
and, below, the theatre.*

*Tel-Aviv: left, the Museum. Above, the
Mann Auditorium, and, below, the beach.*

art and are much in demand by collectors. The old art museum at No. 16 Rothschild Boulevard is Israel's "Independence Hall", for it was here on May 14, 1948, that David Ben Gurion read out Israel's Declaration of Independence, proclaiming the "natural right of the Jewish people to be masters of their own fate, like all other nations, in their own sovereign state."

The city's cultural complex includes also the campus of Tel Aviv University, north of the Yarkon River. Israel's newest museum, dedicated to preserving the memory of the Jewish communities in the Diaspora, many now vanished, is one of the unique attractions on the campus.

There sometimes seems to be a national psychosis on the subject of education. More than 50,000 students are enrolled at the country's seven institutions of higher learning, but to judge from the multiplicity of other schools, academies, colleges and seminaries almost everyone seems to be studying something. The Israeli is a perpetual student. Adult courses abound. And from the open windows of the homes in Tel Aviv streets one hears the squeaking of fiddles and the trills on piano keys as little Israelis struggle manfully to become Yehudi Menuhins or Artur Rubensteins.

Most of the newspapers of the country are published in Tel Aviv, including some 23 dailies, not only in Hebrew, but also in a dozen other languages including English, Spanish, French, Russian, Roumanian, German, Hungarian, Polish and Arabic. For the highly literate population there are some 65 weeklies and 150 fortnightlies or monthlies. The newsstands likewise offer a broad display of the press and magazines from all parts of the world, read here by an intellectually hungry population. The big city is also the center of the book publishing industry, and more than 3,000 titles are published each year. Literature means language. One of the miracles of Israel has been the revival of the ancient Hebrew tongue. Less than a hundred years ago Eliezer Perlman took in hand the ancient speech of the patriarchs and the prophets and painstakingly wrote a new lexicon. He coined new words so that Hebrew could be used in daily speech. Symbolically, he changed his own name to a Hebrew one, Eliezer Ben Yehuda. Many Jews coming to Israel have likewise Hebraized their names. Today the universities teach nuclear engineering, electronics and the computer sciences in the old/new language. Little wonder that practically every city and town in the country has a Ben Yehuda street.

Culture spills over into entertainment. Jaffa at one end, and the old Tel Aviv port area at the other end have become the centres of night life. Along Dizengoff Road are rows of cafes, sprawling out onto the sidewalk, almost with an eye cocked at the Champs Elysées. The recreational interests of the Israeli run to sport as well, and a good Saturday afternoon soccer game will turn out a crowd of thousands. The teams which constitute the several soccer leagues belong to clubs which were originally political in their affiliation, and some still retain considerable elements of such political loyalties. The competition between teams of Hapoel, Betar or Maccabi are accompanied by occasional fierce displays of fanatical support. Israelis, or the visitors, have at their disposal a modern golf course at Caesarea where it is not surprising to find that a divot may expose a fragment of Roman glass. The beaches, the tennis courts, the swimming pools are generally filled. The country has come a long way since

Left, the 32-story Shalom Tower, in Tel-Aviv. Right, a corner of old Jaffa.

the days when young David slung a flat stone and felled his Philistine opponent.

Tourists in Tel Aviv spend the major part of their time at or near hotel row. This spreads up and down the length of Hayarkon Street, which more and more begins to resemble the Miami Beach waterfront. The yacht marina provides berths for a wide variety of small craft. Tel Aviv had made previous efforts to turn its eyes seaward. In 1936, when the port of Jaffa was paralyzed by strikes of the Arab dockworkers and fishermen, it was decided not to permit this vital element of the national economy to remain in Arab hands. Amidst great enthusiasm funds were raised and the north coast of Tel Aviv, near the mouth of the Yarkon River, was proclaimed a port. It was short-lived. The shore was not suitable, and mariners preferred the safety and convenience of Haifa. Even the attempt to establish fishing villages up and down the coast petered out, and fishing concentrated on the main ports, with one important exception. Experiments at raising carp in artificial ponds have proven highly successful, and the northern and central plains area is today dotted with scores of such ponds.

For years Israel's biggest city spread out horizontally only. A few years ago the 32-story Shalom Tower office building created a precedent which is now rapidly being followed, and the high rise buildings are multiplying like mushrooms after a damp night in an Israel pine forest. There are blocks and blocks of white apartment houses, some in good taste, some not.

Headquarters of the Israel Labor movement is in Tel Aviv. Labor is strong in Israel. It is organized in the Histadrut, the Israel Federation of Labor, which is more than a trade union. It also operates some of the major heavy industries in

the country, includes a giant cooperative agricultural distributing system, and provides the health
and medical needs of a great majority of the population. Its building, on Arlosoroff Street, is
occasionally referred to as the Kremlin, sometimes
in jest, sometimes in earnest.

The large metropolitan area around Tel Aviv is
composed of towns with such colorful names as
Garden Heights (Ramat Gan), Gateway to Hope
(Petach Tikva) and Daughter of the Sea (Bat
Yam). Some of these towns are little more than
residential suburbs of Tel Aviv. Others have
developed characters of their own. Herzlia and
Kfar Shmaryahu contain many lovely homes and
villas of the diplomatic corps. Natanya, named
for the American philanthropist, Nathan Strauss,
is also a popular seaside resort. Some towns
had their beginnings in the Jewish volunteers
from overseas who in 1917 and 1918 joined
the 38th, 39th and 40th Royal Fusiliers of the
British Army so they would have an opportunity
to fight for liberation of Palestine from the Turks.
There were also hopes they would be the
nucleus of a Jewish fighting force in their own
country. The British dissolved the Legion after
the war, and many of the men elected to remain
in Palestine. They helped found such townships
as Herzlia, Raanana and Avihail, some more
successful than others. Ramat Gan has se-
cured its position as the diamond center of Israel,
and though all the raw diamonds are imported,
the skills of Israel's workmen have established the
country as a major factor in the world industry.

The architecture of the country ranges from dull
and unimaginative to highly original and in cases
even revolutionary. Refugee architects in the
1930's introduced the style then coming into
prominence in Central Europe, but as it turned

out not always suitable to the sub-tropical climate
of Israel. Arab homes were generally considered
unattractive, and the modern architects turned
up their noses. They soon learned that the small
windows were ideal for keeping out the hot rays
of Israel's long summer, and the Arab homes were
more liveable than the European style villas, with
their big French windows. Newcomers to the
country also learn rapidly that during the *hamsin,*
the hot dry winds that sweep in from the desert,
one does not throw open the windows of one's
home to get more air. To the contrary, the proper
procedure is to close the windows to keep out
the dry air and to preserve within the house what-
ever coolness and humidity may be there. Within
the limitations of their new experlence the
modern architects now experiment with unique
forms. Igloo-shaped homes are not at all uncom-
mon. In the luxury villa suburb of Savyon is a near
faithful reproduction of the White House in
Washington.

Outside the big cities one becomes aware of
the solar hot water heaters which dot the rooftops.
An Israel contribution to help meet the energy
problem, at least in part, these glass absorption
panels draw their heat from the rays of the sun,
and provide the average household with an almost
constant supply of hot water to meet normal
family needs.

Away from the Tel Aviv vortex is Rehovot, site
of the Weizmann Institute of Science, the grave
of Chaim Weizmann, first President of Israel, and
the Weizmann Home. Both of the latter are now
national shrines. The international airport which
bears the name of David Ben Gurion, the country's
first Prime Minister, and regarded by many as the
creator of the State, is east of Tel Aviv. Most
incoming and outgoing planes fly over the city.

Astride the ancient road which traditionally led from Jaffa to Jerusalem are the twin cities of Lydda (Lod in Hebrew) and Ramla. Lydda was a center of Jewish scholarship and culture in the days of the Romans and became the capital of the region under Byzantine rule. Later it was a Crusader stronghold and finally fell into the hands of the Moslems. Ramla was founded by Suleiman in the eighth century and went through a similar chain of events. One interesting sight here is the 14th century Mameluk White Tower, quite visible as a major landmark. Another is little known. In the eighth century Haroun El-Rashid (of 1001 Nights fame) built an underground cavern to store drinking water piped from distant wells for the population of Ramla. Christian pilgrims later named the place for St. Helena, mother of the Christian Emperor, Constantine. Today a persistent visitor can descend into the Pools of St. Helena and row a boat under the vaulted ceilings of the dim and exotic underground chambers.

A little further along the highway one comes to the ancient valley of Ayalon, where Joshua commanded the sun and the moon to stand still until the children of Israel had completed the defeat of their enemies, the Amorites. Today it is site of a lovely national park. Nearby is the Latrun Monastery of the Trappist monks, famous not only for their silence, but also for the excellent wine produced from their vineyards.

One of the more recent attractions is the stalactite cave, small but dazzling in its beauty. Entirely different are the enormous Bet Govrin caves, excavated in the soft limestone hills centuries ago for reasons which are not yet altogether clear. It is easy to get lost in these caves, which are many hundreds in number.

The Judean foothills are not far off. The old road up into these hills through Shaar Hagai (Bab el Wad to the Arabs) was the only access to Jerusalem when the city was besieged in 1948. Israel armored cars, loaded with food supplies and defense materials for the beleaguered population, ran the gauntlet of fire through the narrow, winding highway. Many never made it, and the hulks of their wrecked cars have been left at the roadside in stark testimony to the courage of the brave drivers who manned them. Realistic monuments like these can sometimes be misunderstood. In the early 1950's a U.S. Senator on a fact-finding tour recommended back to Washington that all further aid to Israel should be halted. He testified that he had seen both agricultural and military equipment abandoned and rusting on the sides of the road!

In Israel there are times to be sad and times to rejoice. Holidays and holy days have an influence on the life of the country almost all year around, since the special occasions of the three major faiths are observed by the respective groups in the population. Friday is the Moslem weekly day of rest. Saturday is the Jewish Sabbath. Stores and offices everywhere are closed, and the pace slows down. In the orthodox neighborhoods even the streets are closed to traffic; elsewhere, less observant Jews use the day of rest for outings to the beach or the mountains. On Sunday life resumes at full pace. Schools, offices, stores, public transport all treat this as a normal weekday. Only Christians mark Sunday as their day of rest. Major holidays are sectarian. Christmas is felt little in most of Israel except in the Christian centers, and especially in Bethlehem. At Easter there are church processions in the streets of Jerusalem. Ramadan is the Moslem holy month

Israel's agriculture is characterized by extremes, with tropical fruit grown in Lush valleys, citrus on the plains, and cold weather crops in the mountains.

during which all devout members of the faith fast during daylight hours. The booming of cannon announce the beginning of the fast. Id El Fitris is a three day fast immediately after the Ramadan. There is also a festival on the birthday of the Prophet.

Solemn days in the Jewish calendar are: Yom Kippur, the Day of Atonement, during which the entire country comes to a standstill; even restaurants and hotel dining rooms in the Jewish areas are closed, and non-Jewish visitors are warned to make advance preparations for food; Holocaust Day, and Memorial Day for those who fell in the country's wars. The gayest holidays are Israel Independence Day, marked by parades, festivals and street dancing; Purim, a minor festival, but much given to promenading by children in diverse and imaginative costumes; Chanukah, the Festival of Lights, during which candles are lit for eight

days to mark a Maccabean miracle. Passover, the Festival of Freedom, marks the Exodus from Egypt. The unleavened matza becomes a staple fare in all Jewish homes and restaurants; bread is available during the week only from Arab bakers, and that is usually the dry Arab pitta. Since both Jewish and Moslem holidays are determined in accordance with the lunar calendar, their dates do not coincide with fixed dates on the Gregorian calendar.

In the very center of the country is the area rich in Biblical associations known as Judea and Samaria. In political parlance it has been termed the West Bank (of the Jordan River) or the occupied territories. Originally part of Palestine, this section was occupied by Jordan when the state of Israel was set up, and remained in Jordanian hands until the Six Day War of 1967. Legally it is "occupied". Jordanian law still applies here, and the residents are not citizens of Israel. There is a considerable degree of local municipal self-government. Major cities are: Ramallah, just north of Jerusalem, mostly Christian, and a pleasant urban center for the surrounding countryside. Nablus is the largest city, known to the Jews as Shechem, dating back to Canaanite days and mentioned frequently in the Bible. Nablus was built by Titus soon after the destruction of the Temple in the first century, and was named Flavia Neapolis. The latter name became Nablus. Many Arabs find it difficult to pronounce the letter "p". Etymologists who replace the "b" with a "p" in Arab place names frequently reveal familiar identifications in this way. Nablus is at the foot of Mt. Grizim, holy mount of the Samaritan sect, an offshoot of Judaism. The sect preserves many of the old Jewish customs and ceremonies, but has been completely separatist for two millenia. Today they are sadly reduced to but a few hundred, but still carry on their colorful rites as in the days of antiquity. Outstanding among the many striking remains is Sebastia, where Herod's forum is but one aspect of the great city that once stood here. Much of the West Bank is up in the hills and is largely populated by Arabs. The watershed slopes west to the coastal plain, where Jewish settlements are concentrated, and east down to the Jordan Valley rift along which Israel has built a chain of several dozen farm villages, for defense purposes, and politically to establish the Israeli presence.

Israel's newest port is to be found at Ashdod, some 18 miles (30 kilometers) south of Tel Aviv. Historically this was one of the great Philistine centers, but after the Roman period it disappeared from the map until the 1960's when the Israelis built jetties out into the sea, deepened the waters, and transformed it into a thriving, bustling maritime center, second only to Haifa.

A bit further down the coast is Ashkelon. This, too, had been a Philistine stronghold and site of one of Sampson's exploits. It was besieged by Sargon and Sennacherib, was conquered by Alexander the Great, and continued to flourish under Roman control. It underwent Arab and then Crusader rule, finally passing into oblivion, except for legend and tradition. In 1953 foundations were laid for a new, modern city which now boasts of industries, resort hotels, summer homes and a growing population.

Ashkelon: facing and below, Roman ruins. Right, gardens at the seaside.

5.

About half the land area of Israel is desert, covering much of the southern and eastern parts of the country. This is where Israel sees its greatest opportunities for the future. David Ben Gurion constantly pleaded with the youth of the country to go south, and when he retired from the premiership in 1963 he set the example by taking up residence in a simple hut in the kibbutz of Sdeh Boker, located in the Negev, the southern desert. In the years that ensued others followed, but not in the numbers he had hoped.

The unofficial but recognized "capital" of the Negev is Biblical Beersheba, where Abraham made his covenant, and his son Isaac dug wells, and Jacob pitched his tent. It remained a small town for centuries until taken by the Israel forces in 1948. It has since become a major urban center, with its own luxury satellite, Omer.

Ben Gurion University of the Negev, located here, specializes in those disciplines which can help conquer the desert and make it a productive and profitable area. A nearby war memorial, unique in design, attracts much attention.

The Bedouin camel market in Beersheba is not what it used to be. For one thing, more and more of the desert mariners are settling down to fixed pastoral homes in various parts of the country. The hardy jeep and command car have also

Left, view of the Negev Desert and, below, the Canyon of Invocations.

Facing, another view of the Negev. Bottom, the Red Canyon and, right, King Solomon's Mines.

joined the nomad desert fleets. From Beersheba the road leads straight south into the heart of the Negev. Ben Gurion's hut at Sdeh Boker has become a national monument. The patch of green here, surrounded by sere brown of the desert, is striking, but typical of dozens of others to be seen on the long trek south.

It is an oversimplification to say that Israel has a chronic water shortage. As a matter of fact there is a surplus of water in the north, and the problem is to bring it south where it is needed. For this a National Water Carrier has been constructed, and millions of gallons are sent through pipe lines, or siphoned over deep valleys, or flushed through open ditches from the north, where the Sea of Galilee serves as a reservoir, down to the Negev where much of it is stored in aquifers, nature's own underground cavities for water storage. If water is precious, care must be taken to use it prudently in irrigation. The attractive overhead sprinkler system is considered wasteful, because in the hot summer days much of the sprinkled water evaporates before it reaches the ground. Ditch irrigation is easy where water is plentiful, but the plants are in this way provided with much more water than they can absorb, and the rest is wasted. As a result the Israelis have developed a new system of drip irrigation via pinpoint holes in lengths of plastic piping. The water supply can be scientifically controlled to provide just as much moisture as may be needed, no more and no less. Going a step further, the Israeli farmer can also introduce carefully measured amounts of liquid fertilizer into this water. Thus science reaches new heights of efficiency and economy in its application to agriculture. Still another innovation is the use of plastic sheeting to protect young plants against the burning sun, or to keep out the

54

frost, or to keep in the moist air. From a distance the fields of plastic look almost as if they were snow-covered.

At first sight the desert and the mountain badlands seem completely uninhabitable. How can anyone live where there is no water and almost no rainfall? Yet the archeologists have pinpointed sites where the ancients had a flourishing civilization in a climate not too unlike that of our day. Shivta (Subeita), southwest of Beersheba, was founded by the Nabateans in the First Century and existed through Byzantine times. The population was estimated at about 5,000, and they cultivated extensive fields. Even earlier there was a large city at Avdat. In both places the remaining ruins give evidence of a once prospering community. How did they do it? There are clear traces of dams, irrigation ditches, water reservoirs and other devices to channelize and preserve every drop

of water available. If the Nabateans could do it, the Israelis vowed they could too—and the result is the chain of settlements which now break the desert monotony of the Negev and create man-made oases.

This is not the only instance where archeology has been turned to practical use. In Israel's War of Independence, an Israeli general turned his knowledge of archeology to good use when he followed the track of an ancient Roman road in the Negev, known only to him, and was able to come up in surprise behind the invading enemy force. Others still scour Biblical references in the search for oil. Findings at some of the digs have pointed to the existence of nearby mineral resources. Every Israeli is an amateur archeologist, and almost every home has one or more rocks with historical associations. The laws are rather strict against unauthorized digs, and antiquities

Above, Eilat (Jordanian Aqaba in the distance). Right, the seaside at Eilat. Bottom, Israeli fishermen in the Gulf of Eilat.

are regarded as part of the national wealth of the country.

At the tip end of the Negev is the port of Eilat, providing Israel with its waterway outlet to the Red Sea, the Persian Gulf and the Far East. The ideal climate has made Eilat a favorite winter resort for tourists from northern Europe. In summer it is hot. The shortage of water is overcome, in part, by a local desalination plant operating under Israel patents. The city at the head of the Red Sea in modern times was Aqaba, now on the Jordan side of the line. When the Israelis extended the southern limits of their state down to the Red Sea in 1949 they began to build a new city on the bare shore. This is now Eilat. In the intervening years Eilat has suffered from schizo-

phrenia. Subject to circumstances beyond its control, it still cannot decide whether to concentrate on tourists, for whom many hotels have already been built, or seek to develop commerce and industry, for which there is a deep water port, an oil pipe line and colonies of oil tanks. The two somehow do not go together. In the meantime Eilat has built an airport, and the natives say: Just wait till the railroad reaches here from the north. The crystal clear sea, the underwater beauties of gorgeous coral and a wealth of exotic, colorful tropical fish have made Eilat an attraction for skin divers from everywhere. More recently an underwater observation station has brought these sights within view of all visitors.

The road up back north traverses the lowest

Left, another view of King Solomon's mines, in the Negev. Right the astonishing caves known as the Pillars of Solomon.

level of the Great Rift. This area is known as the Aravah, the Wilderness, and there are indeed, long stretches of wild desert. There are also breaks in the monotony because of natural topographical features, historical sites or oases newly exploited. Among the popular, eye-catching sights are the so-called Pillars of Solomon, about 16 miles (25 kilometers) north of Eilat. These are columns of Nubian sandstone created in the hills by centuries of erosion in several canyons which carry raging flash floods on the one or two occasions a year when rain falls. The hand of man, neither of Solomon nor anyone else, had nothing to do with their creation. Nearby at Timna, however, are copper-bearing strata which were worked by the ancients and perhaps in the time of Israel's Kings as well. There is therefore some justification to call these King Solomon's Copper Mines. Strip mining and later underground mining provided Israel with a modest source of copper cement which was exported for further refining and beneficiation. Production was expensive, and when copper prices on the world's markets dropped, the mines closed.

The list of new, young villages along the Aravah, going north, can be ticked off, but their number increases as new scientific methods discover hitherto unknown and untapped sources of fresh water. Eilot, Samar, Yotvata, Grofit, Ketura, Yahel, Tsafar, En Yahav... each is an outpost of civilization along the bottom of the rift. The warm climate all year around enables the young farmers here to harvest vegetables, flowers and other crops and fly them into European markets when such items are otherwise scarce.

Even in the midst of the Negev, off the major road, mining and industrial developments have made possible creation of townships like Yeruham

61

Above and below, two views of the Dead Sea and, facing, the strange ravines of Neveh Zohar on its shores.

Above and below, two views of curious crystal formation on the Dead Sea.

and Mizpe Ramon where one would never expect to see a sign of life.

The further north one goes, the deeper drops the rift until at last one reaches the shores of the Dead Sea, the lowest spot on the face of the earth, some 1300 feet (400 meters) below the level of the Mediterranean. The Dead Sea is about 50 miles (80 kilometers) long and about 10 miles (17 kilometers) wide. The water contains a 25 to 30% concentrate of various minerals such as calcium chlorides, magnesium, sodium, bromine, potash and others. The Dead Sea Works, located at Sodom at the southern end of this inland body of water, produces mainly potash, most of which is exported.

The name of Sodom of course conjures up images of the wicked city of the Bible. There is much in the landscape which appears to confirm the utter desolation which overtook the place. Rapid evaporation and erosions have resulted in creation of strange salt pillars, one or more of which are pointed out as Lot's Wife. In the water, dwarf pillars of salt rise above the surface, little saline islets.

In the Middle Ages this was known as Mare Asphaltides (Sea of Asphalt) because chunks of the pitch would frequently float to the surface. Geologically this was no surprise, and in recent times prospectors have been encouraged to seek here for oil. None of commercial value has been found, but natural gas produced from a local well provides power for some of the installations in the area. Throughout recorded history the Dead Sea has been the object of scientific curiosity. In our time it is being exploited not only for its rich minerals, but also for features which make it an unusual tourist attraction. Medical evidence has confirmed the therapeutic value of the waters both of the sea and of the rich springs which empty into it. Psoriasis has been found to be especially responsive to treatment here. Furthermore, the rays of the sun are filtered through additional layers of atmosphere before reaching land surface, and their intensity is thereby reduced. It is not easy to get sunburned. There are comfortable, modern hotels at places like Ein Bokek and Ein Geddi oases, but the average tourist passes through quickly. He contents himself with a float on the surface of the water; because of the salt intensity it is impossible to go under (!) and writes a post-card home, postmarked Sodom, to the effect that: "I never thought I'd sink this low."

Because of the constant evaporation in this dry air, exceeding the replenishment of waters brought in by the Jordan River, the level of the Dead Sea is steadily dropping. The authorities are now giving serious consideration to projects which will bring additional water from the Mediterranean to the Dead Sea. One plan calls for a pipe line from a point on the coast almost directly west. The 1200 foot drop down to the Dead Sea would be exploited also for production of power. A more revolutionary plan visualizes a canal from Haifa up the Kishon River to a point in the Jordan River. Ships would be able to sail from the Mediterranean straight inland and to the new sea which would be created as a result of the enlargement of the Dead Sea. The Kingdom of Jordan would be afforded its own outlet to the oceans of the world, and the Dead Sea level would be raised. When it is pointed out that a plan of this nature would require peace in the region, the proponents reply that such a project could help bring peace.

Overlooking the Dead Sea is Masada, site of one of the most stirring events in the long history of the Jewish people. On the top of a massive and

64

Masada: a room in Herod's palace, a stairway of the fortress and the unusual decorations of a wall.

almost inaccessible perimeter of cliff is a large plateau on which, 2,000 years ago, King Herod built fortifications and a lavish summer palace. The clear remains are still to be seen. And here, in 72-73 A.D., the Jewish zealots made their last stand against the Romans. The outlines of the Roman camps which surrounded the besieged mountain for over a year are clearly visible. When it became obvious that there could be no succor, the more than 900 men, women and children decided to commit suicide rather than fall into the hands of the enemy. The dramatic story is recorded in detail by Josephus, and archeological digs on the mountaintop have confirmed each element in his account. Today the name of Masada has become a byword in Israel's history for courage, determination and love of the homeland. In derogatory fashion some refer to the "Masada complex" as stubborness leading to national suicide. Today a cable car provides the visitor with easy access to the top.

Below, the remains of King Herod's palace, atop Ma-sada.

Inland a bit, up in the hills is the new city of Arad, created in 1962 out of nothing. Because of the dry, pollen-free air the place is being promoted as a cure center for sufferers from asthma. Local ordinance even regulates the kind of houseplants which residents may grow. Anything that spreads pollen is banned. Arad is new, clean, well-planned. It has become home for many who do not crave city lights and noise and smog.

The famous Dead Sea scrolls came from many caves in the Judean Desert, but the best known are from the Qumram Caves in the hills overlooking the north end of the Dead Sea. There is evidence of long habitation in these caves, but the last of any consequence was when Jewish freedom fighters, battling the Romans, sought refuge. They kept their archives, daily record books and holy writings as well in clay jars, far back in the caves. These were preserved in the dry desert air until first found by Bedouins and later by archeologists. The Biblical and apocryphal texts are the earliest known versions of these writings, while the secular records cast much light on the daily life of the people. Many of the scrolls are deposited in the Shrine of the Book, at the Israel Museum in Jerusalem.

Much of the Judean hills and the West Bank of the Jordan River were occupied by Israel after the 1967 War and are still administered by Israel. If it is antiquity one is seeking, the place to find it is Jericho. Long, long before Joshua ordered the blasts on the rams' horns and the shouts of the people, creating the decibels which brought down the walls of the city, Jericho had been an inhabited city. It is one of the oldest excavated sites on which human habitations have been found, going back to the year 8,000 B.C. Even pottery had not yet been invented then.

Above, sculpted pillar from the Omayyad palace near Jericho. Right, the building over the tomb of the Patriarchs, Hebron.

The site is a tropical oasis, with ample water, carried in open ditches from the springs to the verdant fields. A more "recent" ruin is that of the winter palace of the Omayyad Khalif Hisham, built in the 8th century. What luxury for those days! It had recessed heating, mosaic floors made to look like carpets, and ornate architectural decorations. It had been in use hardly more than a year or two when it was levelled by an earthquake, and was never rebuilt.

The desert has always had a fascination for many people. Some chose or were compelled to live in caves. And some built their homes in the most inaccessible places, hanging onto rocky cliffs. There are several of the latter in the Judean desert, chief among them the Monastery of St. George in Wadi Quelt. The place was built in the fifth century, destroyed by the Persians in the sixth, rebuilt, later restored by the Crusaders,

abandoned, and repaired again by the Greek monks in the latter part of the 19th century. They have lived there ever since. The Monastery is more easily seen and appreciated from the other side of the ravine.

Life, human as well as vegetable, becomes more normal as one emerges from the tropics of Jericho or the desert of the Dead Sea area, up to and above sea level.

High up, nestling in the hills, is the ancient city of Hebron. The Book of Genesis tells that here Abraham purchased the Cave of Machpela as a burial place for his dead. And here, according to tradition, are the tombs of the Patriarchs and the Matriarchs of the Bible. Legend also places the burial place of Adam and Eve on this site. A church put up here by the Byzantines was later converted into a mosque. For centuries there has been conflict with respect to worship rights in the

70

Left, inside the basilica built at Bethlehem in the place where Christ was born: the precise point of the birth and ceremony. Above, the site and the village of Bethlehem.

building over the cave.

About ten miles (16 kilometers) south of the Holy City of Jerusalem is the little town of Bethlehem. It entered the pages of history when Ruth the Moabitess told her mother-in-law, Naomi, that "thy people shall be my people". Ruth found favor in the eyes of Boaz, the wealthy land-owner, and from their union came the child Oved, who was father of Jesse, who begat David, King of Israel.

It was to Bethlehem that the kings of the East were led when they saw the Star in the sky, and there in the manger was born Jesus Christ. In the close to 2,000 years that followed, both the Grotto and the church above it have undergone numerous changes. The Church of the Nativity is composed of numerous wings which house the various sects that consider the place holy. The

Armenians, the Roman Catholics, the Greek Orthodox and the Anglicans maintain an ecumenical peace, something which has not always been the case here, or at other holy sites in Jerusalem.

Of the three original entrances to the Basilica, two have been walled up. The third is a very low door entering into a narrow passage. One story is that the portal is low so that even the non-believer, on entering, must bow his head. Another source reports that the low entrance was made about the year 1500 so that horses could not be brought into the building. Steps lead from under the High Altar to the Grotto below. A star marks the spot where Jesus was born. Other underground grottoes and chapels are associated with the various events and holy persons in church history. At one end of the Grotto of the Nativity is a cistern. Legend has it that the Star which

כה אמר ה׳ קול ברמה נשמע
נהי בכי תמרורים
רחל מבכה על בניה
מאנה להנחם על בניה כי איננו

led the Wise Men here fell into the water. Look for it, but do not be disappointed, for it is visible only to those who are truly pure at heart!

Bethlehem is a pleasant little town, with a mixed Christian and Moslem population. It offers tourists a wide variety of locally produced souvenirs made in mother-of-pearl, olive wood and local limestone. The entire countryside is filled with interesting sites, some historic, some legendary. Many visitors are fascinated by the Pools of Solomon, three large reservoirs, which in ancient times were the source of water for Jerusalem.

Herod sent water from these pools, by aqueduct, to his fortress on top of the unique, breast-shaped mountain, Herodion.

The road goes on to the legendary Tomb of the Biblical Rachel, who was buried by the side of the road. Together with the Cave of the Machpela, this is the second most holy place for many Jews, after the Western Wall of the Temple. The small domed building over the tomb was erected in the 19th century.

The highway broadens, for now it leads to Jerusalem.

Left, the tomb of Rachel. Above, the sober monument within which lies the tomb. Below, the road followed by Christ on the way from Bethany to Jerusalem.

6.

Jerusalem—in Hebrew, *Yerushalayim;* to the Arabs, *El Kuds* (the Holy).

The holy city of Jerusalem has occupied a central, mystical spot in the affection of a large portion of mankind for many centuries. Philo and other ancients declared it to be at the navel of the world. In Jewish lore it is said there are 70 different names for Jerusalem, all expressing respect and love for the city.

Few cities in the history of man, holy or not, have seen more bloodshed, destruction and ravagement than has Jerusalem, the City of Peace. It has been built, captured, destroyed, rebuilt, razed, built again, dozens of times. It is more than a metropolis. It is a history of mankind, a study in theology in three dimensions, Jewish, Christian and Moslem. It is beyond adequate description for much of it is in the realm of the spirit. It can never be fully seen, for most of it is still buried deep under accumulations of debris.

For centuries pilgrims have come to visit, driven by mystical motivation, and none have gone away without being deeply affected in one way or another. The pilgrims of the twentieth century are no exception. It is an over-simplification to say there are two Jerusalems—the New City and the Old, for in fact there are many Jerusalems, but if we are to avoid being overwhelmed we must indeed simplify. A comprehensive survey of Jerusalem? It has never been done and never will be. The average guide book lists from 200 to 300 sites that "must be seen"

The city on top of the mountains emerged from its stone age anomnymity when it was captured by King David around the year 1,000 B.C. and established as his capital. Here his son, Solomon, built the first Temple on top of what many believed to be Mount Moriah where, in an

Left, a young Israeli in meditation at the Western Wall. Below, "Walk about Zion and go round about her; count the towers thereof. Mark ye well her ramparts, traverse her palaces..." (Psalms).

earlier age, Abraham had been put to the test and had been asked to offer up his son Isaac as a sacrifice to the Lord. The Temple contained the Holy of Holies. To it Jews made their pilgrimages three times a year. Religious Jews everywhere in the world face in its direction when they pray.

A succession of Judean kings ruled here, among them Hezekiah, in whose reign (700 B.C.) a tunnel was bored through solid rock to bring the waters of the Gihon spring to the pool of Siloam in the city. In 1880 discovery was made of an inscription on the walls deep within the tunnel, made by the workmen who had been digging from opposite directions, heard each other's blows from the other side, and finally burst through to meet. The inscription recording this event was removed by the Turks and is today in Istanbul. The adventurous visitor can wade the length of this 1765 foot (535 meter) tunnel, but not in the rainy season when the water is too high.

Jerusalem was destroyed by Nebuchadnezzar, king of Babylon, in 587 B.C. Seventy years later, thanks to Cyrus and Darius, rulers of Persia, some Jews returned and rebuilt their Temple. An historically accurate model (on a scale of 1 to 50) of the Temple and the whole city of Jerusalem as it appeared in the days of the Second Temple, has been constructed on the grounds of the Holyland Hotel.

In 70 A.D. the Romans sacked the city and destroyed the Second Temple. The sole remnant was the high retaining wall of the upper courtyard of Herod's Temple, known for centuries as the Jews' Wailing Wall, but more recently as the Western Wall. For the Jews it is a shrine in which national and religious sentiments are deeply intertwined. After the Dispersion, Jews continued

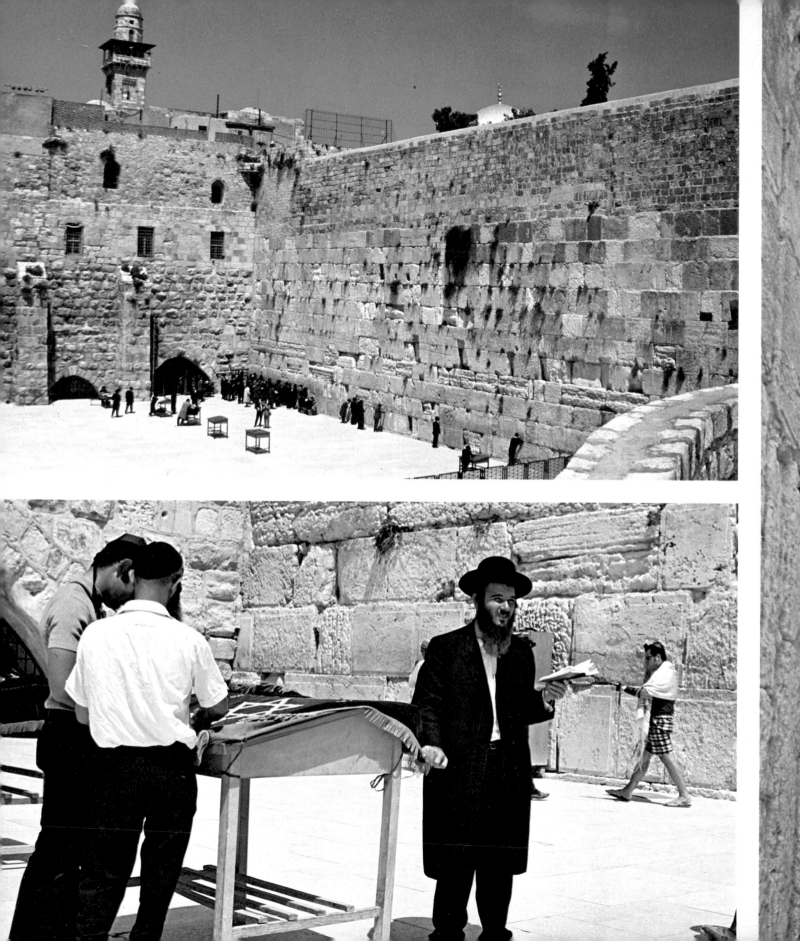

to put Jerusalem at the center of their longings and their liturgy. Through the long years of exile they repeated the pledge: "If I forget thee, O Jerusalem, let my right hand forget its cunning." And in repetition of the words of the Psalmist, they never forgot. This was an emotional-religious-national longing which was at last realized in modern times through Zionism, the national liberation movement of the Jewish people.

The destruction of the Temple had been physical only. The Land of Israel still lived in Jewish history. The capital city itself fell and rose many times under Roman, Byzantine, Persian, Ummayad, Abbasid, Fatimid, Crusader, Mameluk, Ottoman, British, Jordanian and Israel rule. As we have seen, Jewish identification with the city was total and all-embracing, but the Wall was always foremost in its mystical attraction. For many the Tomb of King David on Mount Zion was also held in special reverence. It should be noted that the picturesque Tower of David, almost a trademark of the Jerusalem skyline, has no connection with David, not even in legend. It was built by Herod as a fortification tower, and the Arabs added a minaret.

In recent years intensive archeological excavations have taken place and indeed are still going on. They have exposed more of the walls of the Temple Mount, the entrances to the holy area, the surrounding complex of homes, and commercial premises. The trained eye can read details of history in these stones, some still bearing the carbon black of ancient conflagration, some carefully hewn to fit together as prescribed by an ancient architect. The prayers and legends that bound a people to their past have been sturdily reinforced by this newly uncovered evidence of the glory of Biblical Judea.

Above, view of the Mount of Olives from the Dome of the Rock. Below, the Garden of Gethsemane.

Jerusalem has a sanctity for Christians because many of the major events in the life of Jesus took place here. This was the site of the Last Supper, Gethsemane, the scene of the agony and betrayal, and Golgotha, known also as Calvary. He was crucified and was resurrected here. There are differences of opinion among the various sects and denominations and scholars with respect to some of the holy places. There are at least 17 theories on the actual location of the Holy Sepulchre, but general acceptance is given to the place designated by the mother of the Emperor Constantine, Queen Helena, when she visited the Holy Land in the fourth century.

The Church of the Holy Sepulchre was first built by Constantine in the year 335 A.D. and destroyed by the Persians in 614. Today's building is a patchwork of the various attempts to raze and restore during the 1300 years that followed. As in Bethlehem, the several sects have staked out their rights and their claims in the edifice, and at times the disputes among them have led to public clashes. Represented in the Church are the Franciscans for the Roman Catholics, the Greek Orthodox and the Armenians, as well as the Coptic, Syrian and Ethiopian Churches. The building is almost a maze of chapels and chambers clustered around the Tomb, the 14th Station

The rock of the Agony, in the church built at Gethsemane, and, below, the Via Dolorosa.

of the Cross.

Elsewhere in the city is the Garden Tomb, recognized by some as the authentic sepulchre, with another Golgotha nearby on Skull Hill. The faithful pilgrim will want to follow the Stations of the Cross along the Via Dolorosa, all indicated by sign posts. At the Ecce Homo Arch, where Jesus was shown to the crowd, the sisters of the Sion Convent point out, on a lower level, what is said to be the original cobble-stone Roman pavent where Jesus trod.

On Mount Zion it is easy to get lost among the cluster of buildings in which Christian and Jewish holy spots merge one on the other. Here is the Cenacle, the Room of the Last Supper, the Church and Abbey of the Dormition. Every corner of the Old City has a Christian association.

For the Moslems Jerusalem is the third of their sacred cities, after Mecca, where Mohammed was born, and Medina, where the Tomb of the Prophet is located. In Jerusalem the rock on Mount Moriah is identified in Moslem tradition as the spot from which the Prophet rose to heaven, climbing the rungs of a gold and silver ladder. Over this place the Moslems built their Dome of the Rock, and alongside it the El Aqsa mosque. The entire plateau on which once stood the Temple is now the Haram al-Sharif, occupied by

The Tower of the Holy Sepulchre and the altar situated at the point where Christ's cross was erected. Below, the Orthodox church of Jerusalem.

Moslem buildings. The more pious Jews refrain from entering on the Temple Mount lest they perchance set foot on the Holy of Holies, forbidden to ordinary man. The more nationalistic Jews, on the other hand, seek every opportunity to enter and demonstratively to pray there, to give strength to their historical claim to the place.

The gilt-topped Dome of the Rock is octagonal shaped. The decorations are breathtaking, and for the most part are artistic Arabic calligraphy executed in marble mosaic, glazed Persian tiles and arabesques painted on wood. The stained glass windows and the impressive Corinthian pillars contribute to the solemn beauty. It is called the Mosque of Omar, but was not built by Omar and is not a mosque. El Aqsa has a silver dome, and its decorations too are exquisite. Interestingly, the two buildings are among the oldest in Jerusalem, having survived both earthquakes and wars. Visitors must remove their shoes before entering any Moslem holy place.

The Old City is surrounded by a wall, parts of which were built at different periods. As we see it today it is the work of the Turkish Sultan, Suleiman the Magnificent, from the middle of the 16th century. Entrance into the Old City is though gates of varying degrees of splendor. Originally they were for defense, and often had a drawbridge dropped over a surrounding moat. The more spectacular entrances are:

Damascus Gate, called by the Jews Shaar Shechem, and by the Arabs, Bab el Amoud. This was long considered to be the principal gate of entry, and the crowned heads of Europe, on their visits to the Holy Land, usually made their entrance here. One striking exception is noted below.

The "Old City" of Jerusalem. Left: Salomon's Platform, known today as the Haram Esh Sharif. Bottom, a camel in the streets of the city and an Arab coffeehouse. Facing and below: Two aspects of the "bazaar".

Some of the most famous gateways of Jerusalem. Facing: Herod's Gate. Right: The Golden Gate and next the New Gate. Bottom: The Damascus Gate.

Jaffa Gate, known to the Arabs as Bab el Khalil, Gate of the Friend (the Patriarch Abraham) is adjacent to the Citadel of David. The road to the right leads to the Armenian quarter; the opening to the left into the Christian quarter, and the alley going straight ahead leads into the heart of the bazaar. Wilhelm II, on his triumphal visit to Jerusalem in 1898, elected to enter here because he could do so with dignity, though the wall had to be widened to accomodate his carriage.

Zion Gate, called by the Arabs Bab el Nebi (for the Prophet David), leads to Mount Zion. Incidentally, motor vehicles can enter only at Jaffa and Zion Gates, but must then follow a fixed route through the Old City. Other gates, each with its own historic associations, are known as the New, Dung, Golden, Lions (St. Stephens) and Herod Gates. Not all are open.

Between Damascus and Herod Gates is the entrance to strange quarries which penetrate deep under the old walled city for about 200 meters. The Bible tells that when the stone was quarried for the building of Solomon's Temple no one heard the sound of the chipping of the rock. Indeed they could not, for the stones apparently came from this vast cavern which was burrowed completely under the town. The site, also known as the Cave of Zedekiah, has sacred reverence to the Masonic Order, which holds special ceremonies there.

The Old City is not just an historical museum. People live here. The narrow, picturesque streets of the markets are usually crowded with local Arabs shopping for their fruits, vegetables, meat, clothing and other necessities of life, rubbing elbows with tourists for whom the souvenir shops abound. What used to be the old Jewish quarter

In the Valley of the Kidron, the tombs of Bnei Hezir, Zachariah and Absalom.

was left in ruins in 1948 when war cut the city in two, but today that section is being revived on two levels. The archeologists are busily at work probing the depths and uncovering the life of previous millenia. Above ground new synagogues, housing projects and religious academies *(yeshivot)* are multiplying. In some places the scars of the past remain as reminders, like the ruins of the Hurva Synagogue. Elsewhere attempts are made to keep the architecture of the new in conformity with the tone and style of the old city.

Throughout the entire city of Jerusalem, it should be noted, municipal ordinances, first put into effect by the British, require that all buildings must be built with or at least faced with stone. This, too, gives Jerusalem a character of its own, quite different from the modern cities and towns on the coast.

East Jerusalem, which until 1967 had been under Jordanian rule, consists not only of the Old City within the wall, but also of certain quarters north and south of the walls. It is not by accident that the various tombs and burial places are all outside, for ancient custom forbade burials within the cities. Location of a tomb has often helped establish the limits of an ancient town.

There is no end to the tombs: Herod's Family Tomb, Sanhedria Tombs, Tomb of the Kings, Tomb of Absalom, Tomb of the Judges and others. One of the most impressive, though possibly the least visited, is the so-called Tomb of the Kings. Best evidence is that this magnificent complex of burial chambers was constructed by a Jewish Queen Helena (not to be confused with Helena the Christian, mother of Constantine). This Helena was ruler of Adiabene, a small kingdom in Mesopotamia. She and her family came to visit the

Temple about 25 years before its destruction by the Romans. She was no mythical character, and tales of her benefactions are preserved in the Talmud. The ornate sarcophagus which is said to have contained her body was discovered in 1863 and is now in the Louvre. Visitors may wander about in her spacious catacombs by the light of candles or flashlights.

Many of the country's antiquities were long ago looted by invaders or ordinary bandits. The Rockefeller Museum, just outside of Herod's Gate, contains an excellent collection of what had been salvaged and accumulated in the years of British rule. The Israel Museum, the Antiquities Department Museum and others likewise continue to preserve new finds that are being uncovered.

The Mount of Olives is revered as the place of Christ's Ascension, but the church built on the spot was transformed into a mosque. The striking building nearby, with the high square tower, was originally a German hospice, opened in 1910, and named for the wife of Wilhelm II, Augusta Victoria. It later became a Government House and hospital. The classical panorama view of the city of Jerusalem, old and new, is seen from the Mount of Olives. Jerusalem's old Jewish cemetery here, once desecrated, has since 1967 been restored in large part.

Jerusalem is the capital of Israel and the seat of its Government. The major administrative buildings are gathered in a section of the new city known as the Kirya, dominated by the Knesset building, which houses Israel's single house Parliament. Visitors admire the wall tapestries executed by Marc Chagall and the iron gates wrought by sculptor David Palumbo. Many other

Above, one of the modern buildings on the campus of the Hebrew University of Jerusalem.

public buildings are in the same area. The Hebrew University built its new campus here when the original grounds on Mount Scopus were cut off in 1948. The latter have since been restored and expanded. The Israel Museum is a treasure house of art, though most eye-catching are the unique Shrine of the Book, containing the Dead Sea Scrolls, and the surrounding Billy Rose Sculpture Garden.

Mount Herzl is Israel's National Cemetery. Here are interred many of the nation's leaders, chief among them Theodor Herzl, the Hungarian/Viennese visionary who founded the Zionist movement. In 1895 he wrote *The Jewish State,* which called for re-establishment of the Jewish national homeland; in 1897 he summoned the first world Zionist Congress, which began the political action to realize this aim. Herzl died in 1904, but the movement he set up carried on to success. One of his epigrams is regarded almost as a national slogan of Israel: "If you will it, it is no dream."

Yad V'Shem is the awesome memorial to the memory of the 6,000,000 Jews who died in the Holocaust in Europe. The Jewish people have vowed never to forget, but they choose also to remember those who gave help in time of need. The Avenue of the Righteous Gentiles, leading to Yad V'Shem, is a broad, tree-lined boulevard, and the trees are planted by men and women who, at risk of their lives, helped to rescue Jews from the Nazis.

The New City, or West Jerusalem, came into being in 1861 when Jews spilled out from behind the old walls and set up a series of suburbs. The British philanthropist, Sir Moses Montefiore, helped the new settlers, placing at their disposal a generous fund from the estate of the American, Judah Touro. Montefiore also built the windmill, ruined in 1948, but now restored as a museum.

Until the era of modern skyscrapers, the dominant building in the new city was the Y.M.C.A. tower, built in 1933 across the street from the distinguished King David Hotel, site of interna-

tional conclaves and home of visiting royalty. The right wing of the hotel, completely blown up by the Jewish underground in 1946 because it housed the central offices of the Mandatory Government, has been so restored as to show no signs of destruction.

Excellent medical services are available in a number of hospitals which serve Arabs and Jews alike and draw patients from all over the world. Chief among them are the new quarters of the Shaare Zedek Hospital, and the Hadassah Medical Center at Ein Karem. At the latter visitors are attracted by the 12 stained glass windows executed by Marc Chagall in the four walls of the hospital synagogue, and symbolizing the twelve tribes of Israel. In the valley far below are the church and monastery marking the traditional birthplace of St. John the Baptist.

Traversing the residential section of the new city is the Valley of the Cross, deriving its name from the legend that the Cross was cut from a tree here. Busy road traffic passes the Monastery of the Cross, practically hidden in its olive grove. Center of the Israel Chief Rabbinate is a modern

Above, the Parliament, or Knesset; below, the tomb of Theodor Herzl, founder of the Zionist movement, in the national cemetery of Israel:

A statue by the sculptor Antoine Bourdelle in the Israel Museum. Right, the Mill of Montefiore. Next page: the Citadel and the Tower of David in Jerusalem.

building, Hechal Shlomo.

At the western approaches to Jerusalem is the John F. Kennedy Memorial, with a pillar for each of the states in the U.S.

It becomes clear that Jerusalem, while steeped in antiquity and drenched in history, is also very modern and very much alive. It appeals to all senses. Jerusalem is also sounds. At the right time of year one can hear simultaneously the call of the Muezzin from the minarets, the joyful ringing of church bells, and the amplified singing at the Western Wall as the Jews light their Chanukah candles. In the old bazaars it is also a city of intermingled odors, among which the discerning may identify spices and perfumes, burning charcoal, hot Espresso and various indeterminate pungent and acrid scents.

Much of the city's charm comes from its buildings and its ruins—holy, ancient, modern, striking, exotic, but the life of the city is also in its people. This is a truly cosmopolitan city. Between 1948 and 1967 it was cut in two, separated by high wall and barbed wire. Following the Six Day War all walls were removed, and the divided city became one, with freedom of access to the holy places for all. The result is a diverse intermingling of people on the streets, an intermixture of colors, ways of dress, mannerisms and cultures. There are city Arabs and desert Arabs, in western dress or traditional garb. There are Jews of exotic types from Yemen, Bukhara and Russian Georgia. There are Christians from all over the world, and ecclesiastics in the garb of their respective monasteries, convents, orders and sects. There is a babble of many languages. One gets the feeling that this is the crossroads of the world, or perhaps the ancients were right after all when they said that it is the navel of the universe.